THIRD SERIES

# New Classics to Moderns

# 4

# Contents

Yorktown Music Press

Exclusive Distributors:
**Hal Leonard**
7777 West Bluemound Road, Milwaukee, WI 53213
Email: info@halleonard.com
**Hal Leonard Europe Limited**
42 Wigmore Street Marylebone, London, WIU 2 RY
Email: info@halleonardeurope.com
**Hal Leonard Australia Pty. Ltd.**
4 Lentara Court Cheltenham, Victoria, 9132 Australia
Email: info@halleonard.com.au

Order No. YK22143
ISBN 978-1-78305-372-8

Edited by Sam Lung.
Music processing and layout by Camden Music Services.

Printed in the EU.

*www.halleonard.com*

# Toccata in A Minor, SWWV 298

Jan Pieterszoon Sweelinck
1562–1621

**Allegro moderato**

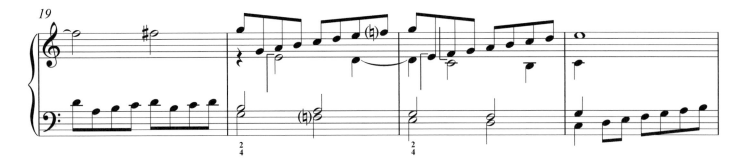

rit.

# Prelude No.11 in F Major

*from* The Well-Tempered Clavier (Book I)

Johann Sebastian Bach
1685–1750

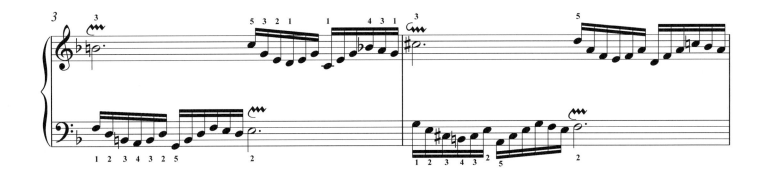

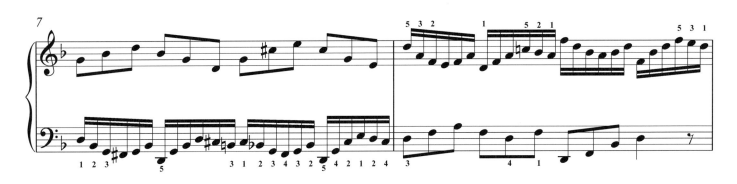

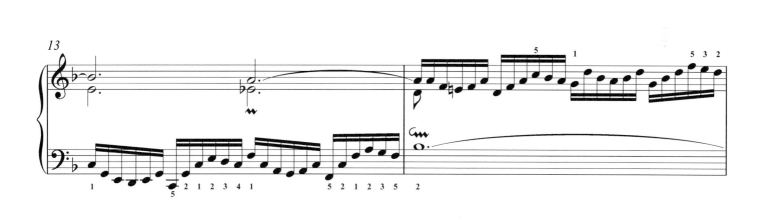

# Allegro

## 3rd Movement *from* Overture No.1, Op.1

Carl Friedrich Abel
1723–1787

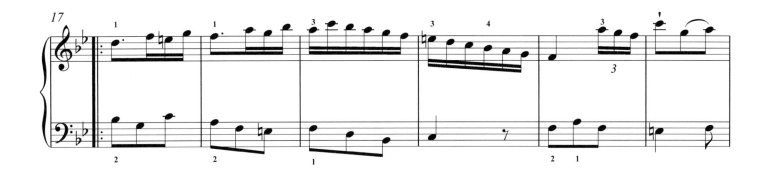

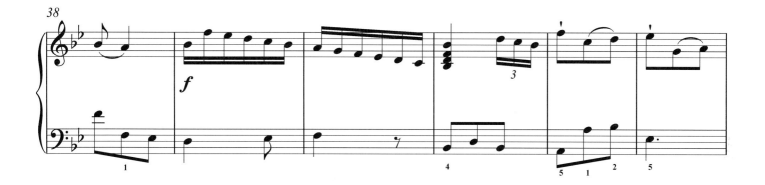

# Gavotte

François Joseph Gossec
1734–1829

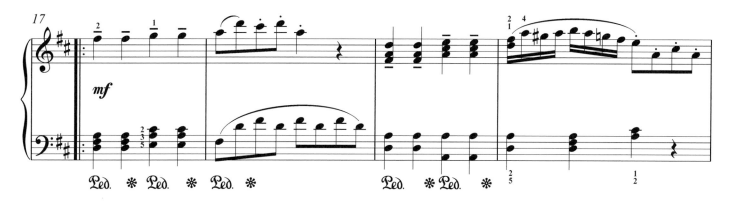

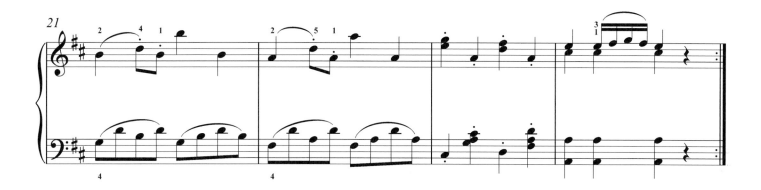

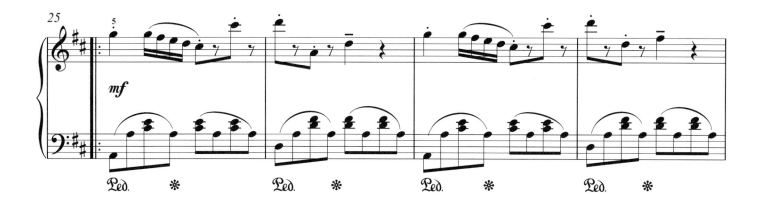

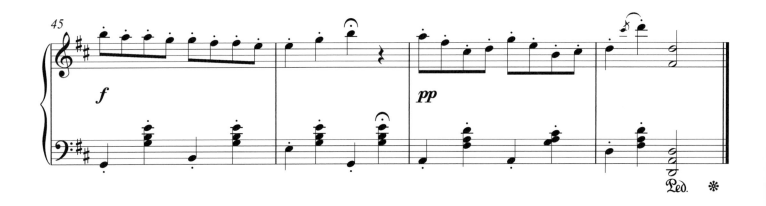

# Andante

*from* Sonata in G Major, Op.79

Ludwig van Beethoven
1770–1827

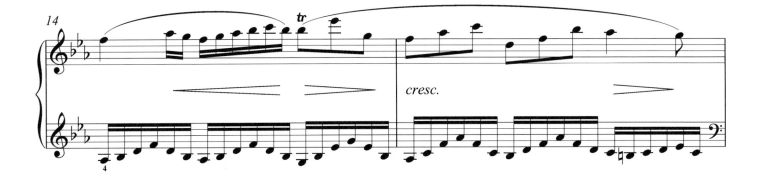

# Winter Morning

*from* Album For the Young

Peter Ilyich Tchaikovsky
1840–1893

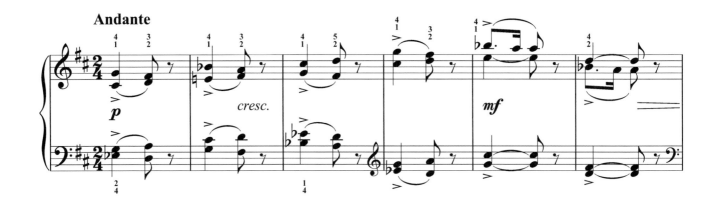

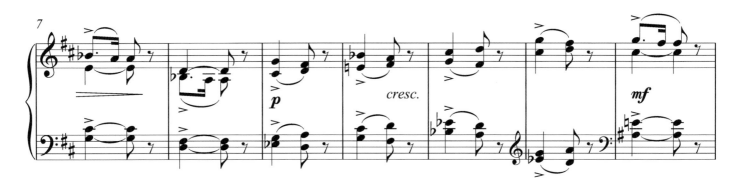

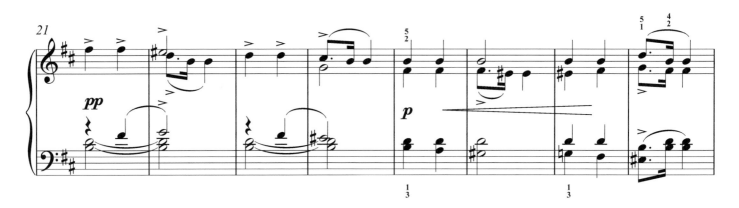

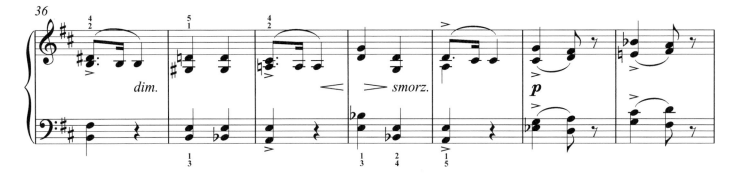

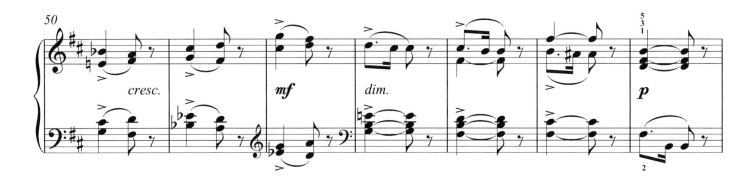

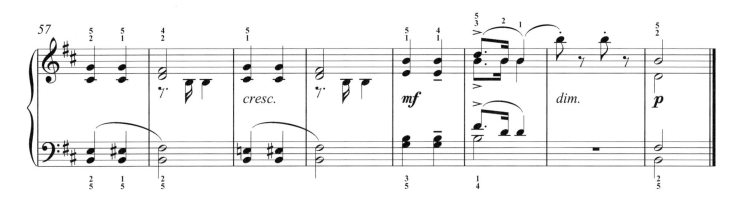

# Piano Music For Young And Old
## No. 14

Carl Nielsen
1865–1931

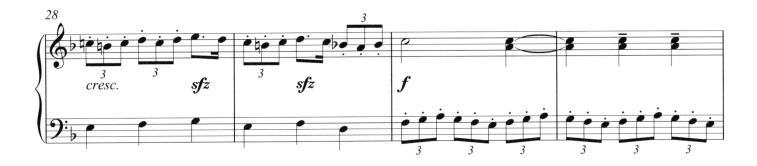

# Pesante

No.8 *from* Les Cinq Doigts

Igor Stravinsky
1882–1971

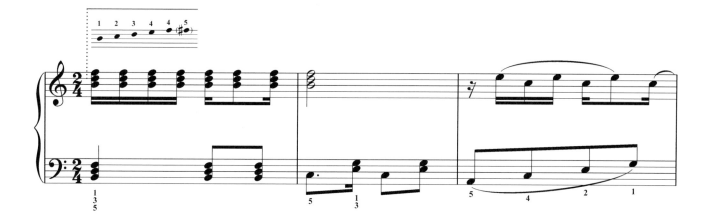

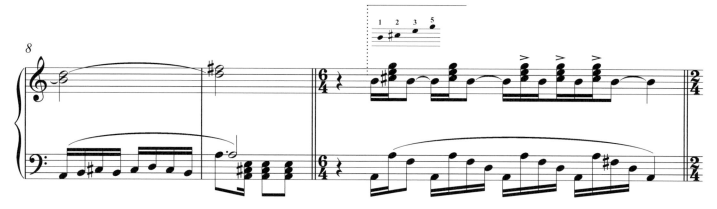

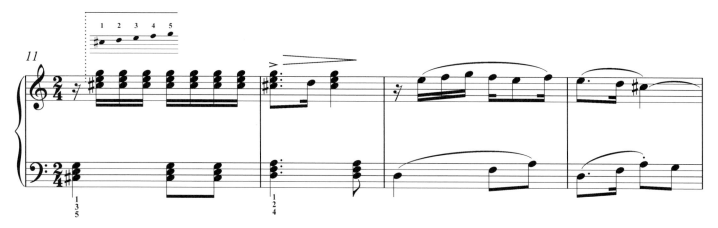

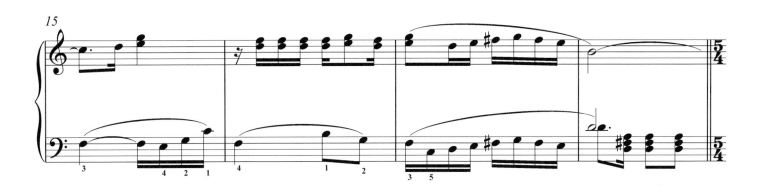

# Two Turtle Doves

*from* Partridge Pie

Richard Rodney Bennett
1936–2012

**Gentle** ♩. = 54

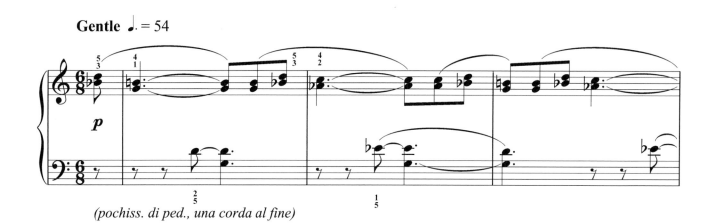

(pochiss. di ped., una corda al fine)

**pochiss. sost.**     **a tempo**

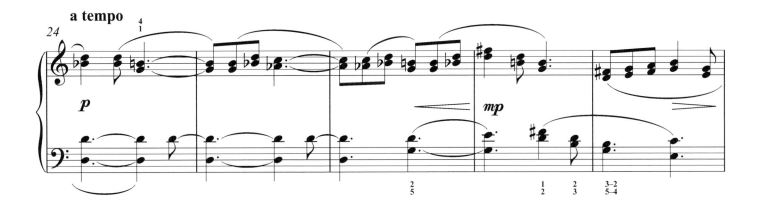

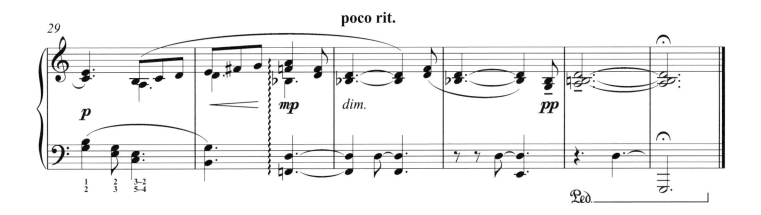

# Spanish Tummy

*from* In The Pink

Brian Chapple
b.1945

Fast (♩ = *c*.168)

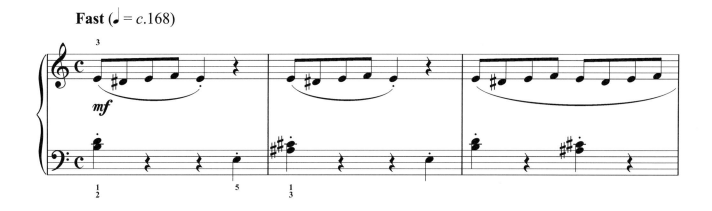

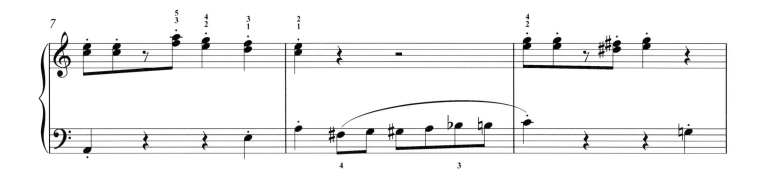

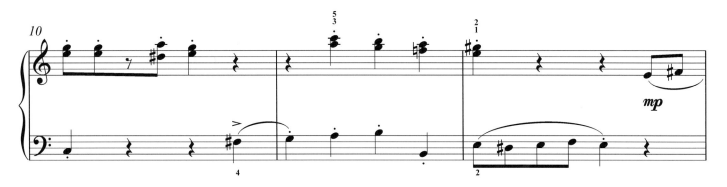

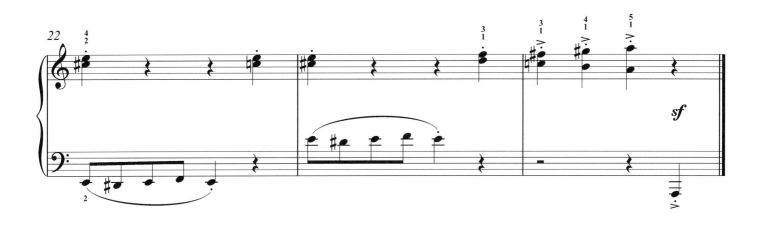

# All Alone

*from* Twelve-O

Robert Walker
b.1946

**Very slow and sustained (adagio sostenuto)**

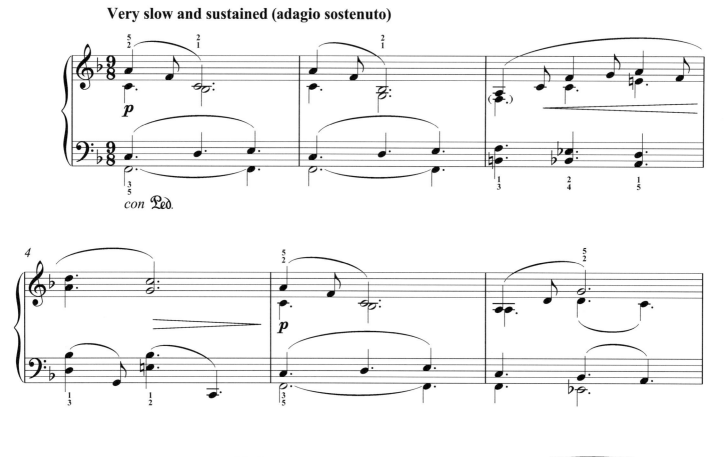

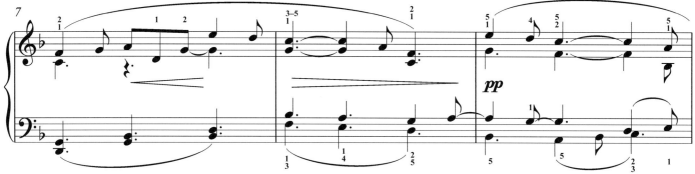

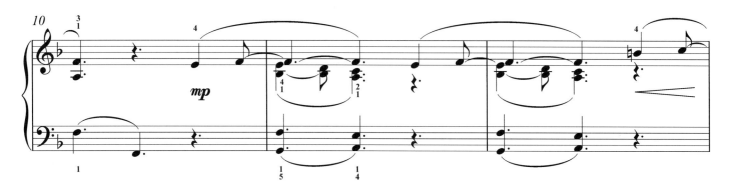

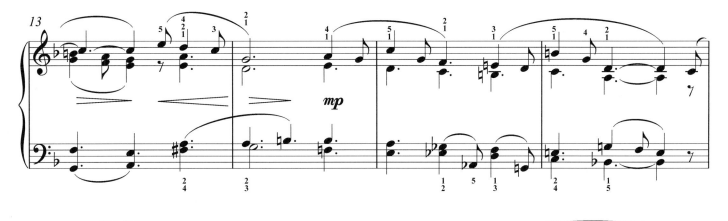

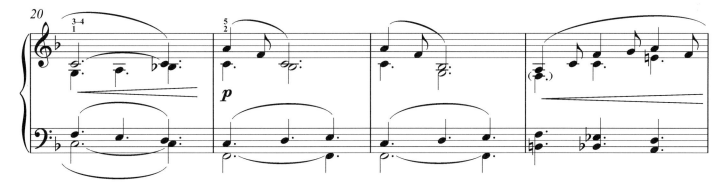

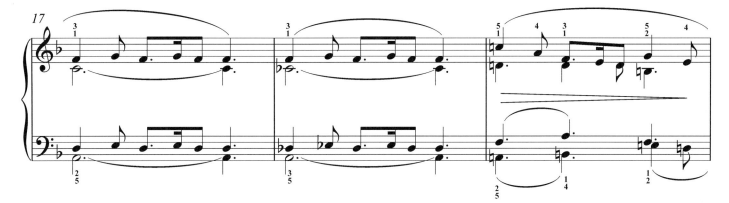

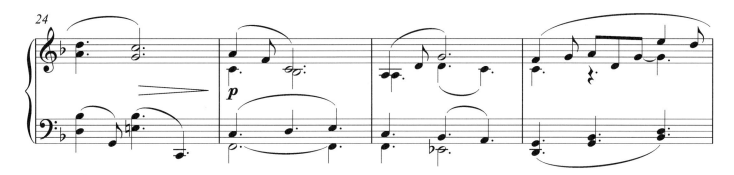

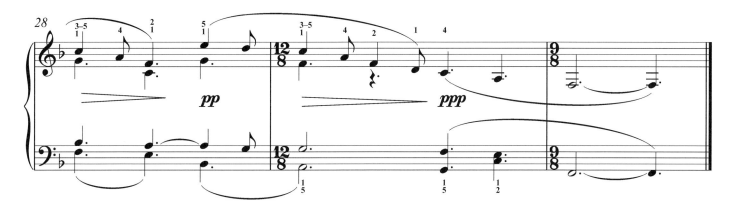

# The Shepherd Girl

*from* Folk Melodies

Witold Lutoslawski
1913–1994

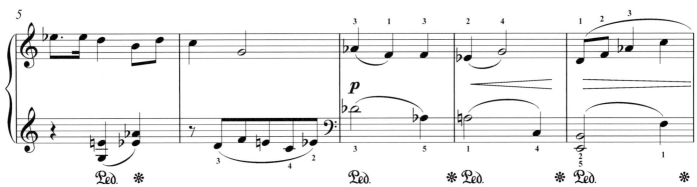

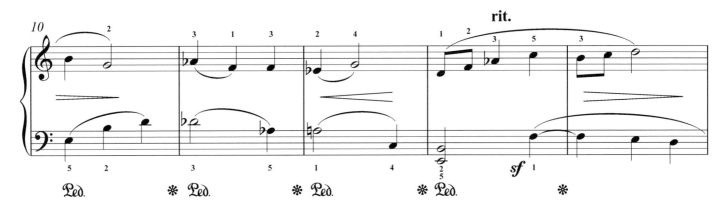

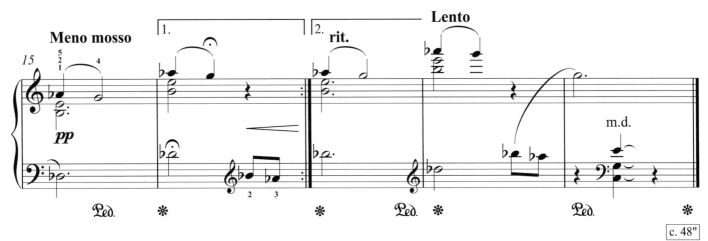

c. 48"

# The Gander

*from* Folk Melodies

Witold Lutoslawski
1913–1994

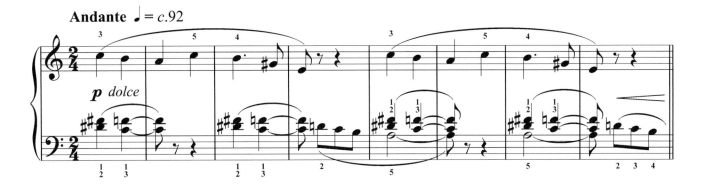

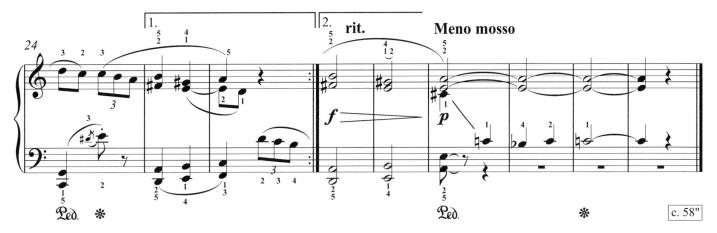

# Snow Prelude No.3

Ludovico Einaudi
b.1955

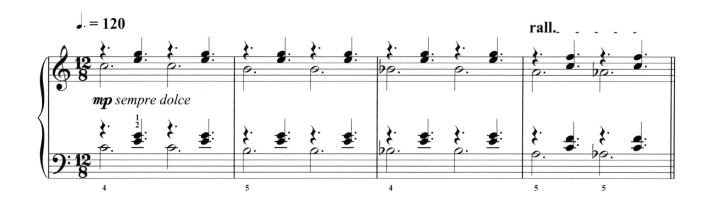

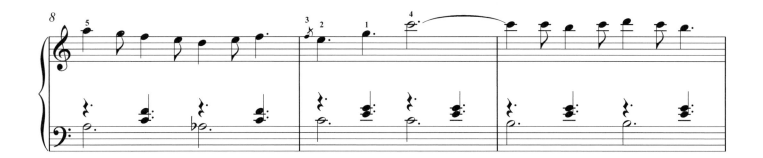

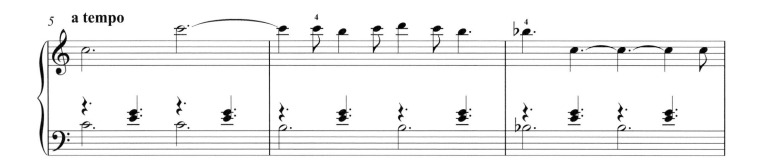

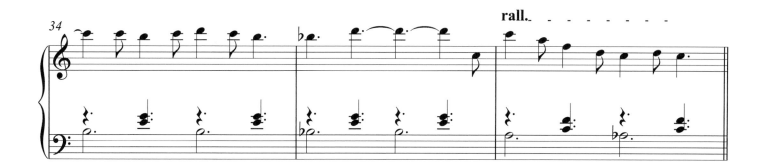

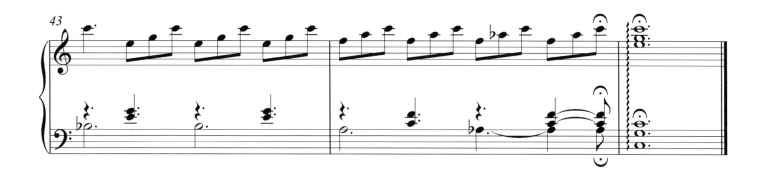